C000148379

DISCOVER &
LEARN

THE SOLAR SYSTEM

by
Gemma McMullen

©2017
Book Life
King's Lynn
Norfolk PE30 4LS

ISBN: 978-1-78637-073-0

Written by:
Gemma McMullen

Edited by:
Grace Jones

Designed by:
Drue Rintoul

CONTENTS

Words in **bold** are explained in the glossary on page 31.

THE SOLAR SYSTEM

The Solar System is the Sun and all of the objects that orbit (move around) it. Eight planets in total orbit the Sun, including the one on which we live, planet Earth. It is not only planets which orbit the Sun, many moons, dwarf planets (see page 20) and asteroids (see page 26) also make up our Solar System. Each of the objects which circle the Sun are held there by a force called gravity.

THE SUN

PLANET EARTH

WHAT IS GRAVITY?

Gravity is what scientists call 'a force
of attraction'. It is a pulling force which is all around
us. We cannot see gravity. All objects pull on each
other. Earth's gravity pulls objects towards its core
(centre), so the objects stay on Earth's surface. So if
we drop something, it will always fall to the ground.

APPLE

GRAVITY

MASS AND DISTANCE

The strength of gravity depends on **mass** and distance. How close objects
are to each other will affect how much pull the force has. For example, the
further that astronauts travel from Earth, the less they are pulled by its gravity.

THE SUN

WHAT IS THE SUN?

The Sun is a star. Stars are giant balls of gas which are very hot and bright. Other stars can also be suns, but our sun is unique to us because we orbit around it. The Sun is very large, but many other stars are larger. The Sun appears as the biggest star to us, because it is the closest star to our planet. From Earth, the Sun appears to be the same size as the Moon, but in fact it is about 400 times bigger.

HOT STUFF!

The Sun lights and heats all of the planets in our Solar System. The temperature at the centre of the Sun reaches over 15 million degrees Celsius, and the Sun is hot enough to melt any known substance. Only a very small percentage of the Sun's heat reaches Earth.

THE EQUATOR

THE EQUATOR

The equator is the imaginary line running around the middle of planet Earth. The power of the Sun is at its strongest along this line because it is the closest point of Earth to the Sun. Therefore, the countries that run along the equator are the hottest on our planet.

CREATING LIFE

All living things need the Sun.
Without the Sun, Earth would
be almost pitch black all of the
time and colder than the coldest
winter imaginable. No plants
would grow, therefore animals
could not feed.

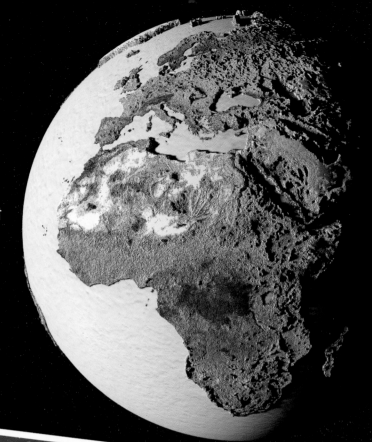

PROTECTION

The Earth is surrounded by a **magnetic field**.
The magnetic field protects us from the Sun's
strong rays. If it wasn't there, Earth would
become too hot and all life on Earth would die!

DOES THE SUN MOVE?

In the morning, the Sun appears to rise, and then to move from east to west during the day. In the evening, the Sun seems to disappear completely. We say that it has 'gone down'. In fact, the Sun does not move at all, but planet Earth does. As well as orbiting the Sun, Earth is always spinning on its own **axis**. When our part of the world is in darkness, the opposite part of the world is lit up because it is facing the Sun.

SOLAR ECLIPSE

About twice every year, the path of the Moon causes it to move in front of the Sun. This is called a solar eclipse. As the Sun's light and heat becomes blocked, a part of Earth becomes dark and cold for a short time. During a total solar eclipse, all that can be seen of the Sun is a halo of glowing gases.

PREDICTIONS

Astronauts can predict the exact time that a solar eclipse will happen and can predict them for many years to come. During a solar eclipse, animals can get confused because they think that night time has arrived.

SUPER SUN!

Stars can be different colours.
The largest stars are blue
or red. Smaller stars like
the Sun, are yellow.

It takes about eight minutes for
the Sun's light to reach Earth.

The Romans called the Sun 'Sol'.
In Ancient Greece, the Sun was called 'Helios'.

In the past, people believed that
the Sun orbited the Earth, rather
than the other way around

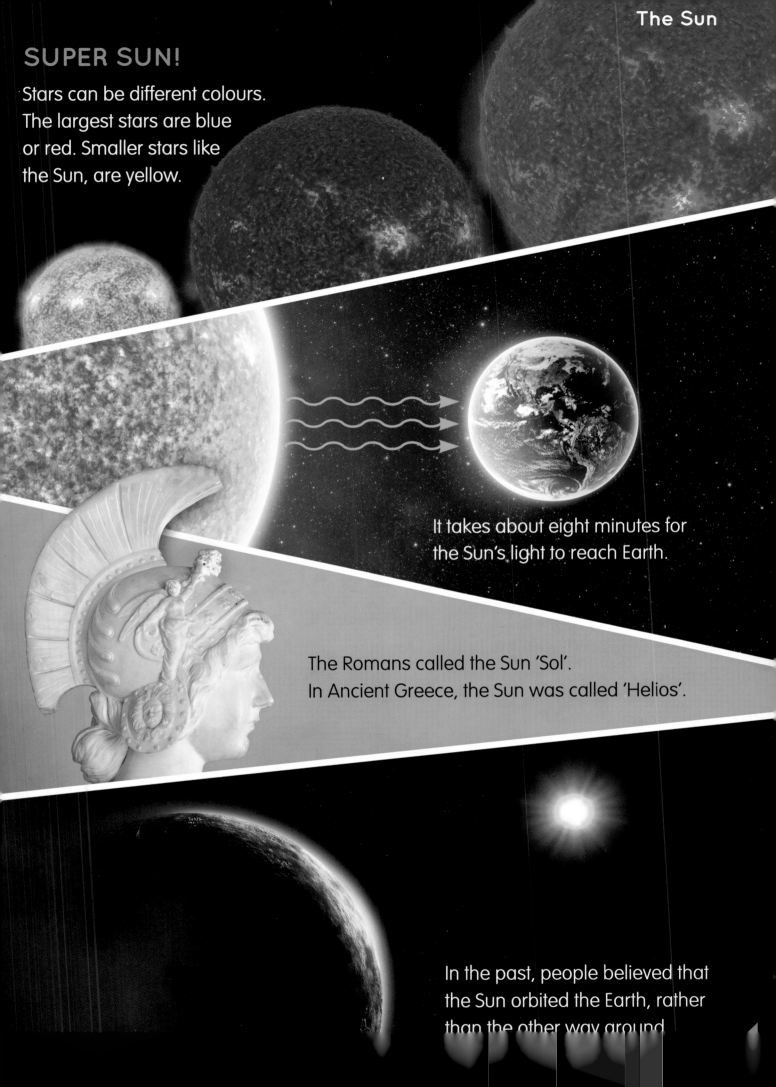

THE MOON

WHAT IS THE MOON?

The Moon is a large ball of rock which orbits planet Earth. The Moon is smaller than planet Earth – about a quarter of its size. The word 'month' comes from the Moon, because the Moon circles Earth about once a month.

THE MOON

THE SURFACE OF THE MOON

The Moon has no life on it. It has a dusty surface that is covered with craters. Craters are huge dents, and were caused on the Moon by massive pieces of rock bashing into it billions of years ago.

CRATER

THE LIGHT OF THE MOON

The Moon has no light of its own. The light that we see at night time is actually the light of the Sun reflected onto the Moon. The same part of the Moon always faces Earth. This means that there is a side of the Moon that we never see.

THE SHAPE OF THE MOON

The Moon is a **spherical** object. It appears to change shape throughout the month. This is due to a smaller or larger part of the Moon being lit by the Sun at one time. In fact, the Moon does not change shape at all.

ASTRONAUTS

Astronauts are the scientists who travel into space. Most astronauts are lucky enough to travel into space in vehicles called space shuttles. They spend a long time training to get used to the feeling of having no gravity as there is very little gravity in space. There are even space stations where astronauts can stay for long periods of time.

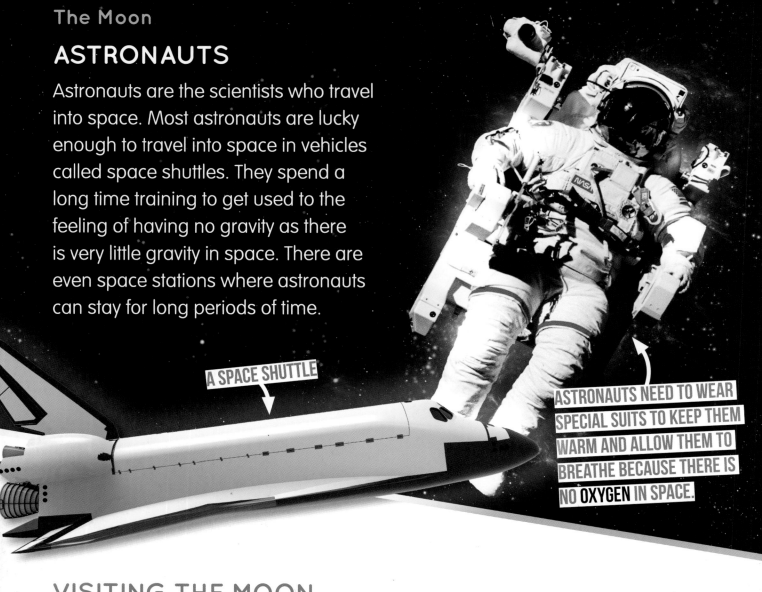

A SPACE SHUTTLE

ASTRONAUTS NEED TO WEAR SPECIAL SUITS TO KEEP THEM WARM AND ALLOW THEM TO BREATHE BECAUSE THERE IS NO OXYGEN IN SPACE.

VISITING THE MOON

Apart from Earth, scientists know more about the Moon than any other object in our Solar System. Astronauts have even landed on the Moon before. In total, 12 people have walked on the Moon.

MAGNIFICENT MOON!

Planet Earth is not the only planet which has a moon. Mars has two moons, Uranus has around 27 moons and both Saturn and Jupiter have over 50 moons each!

PHOBOS

DEIMOS

MARS

Footprints left on the Moon by astronauts are still there.

The Romans called the Moon 'Luna'. The Ancient Greeks called the Moon 'Selene'.

The Moon is very hot during the day but very cold at night.

THE PLANETS

WHAT ARE THE PLANETS?

The planets are the largest objects to orbit the Sun. They are made from rock or gas. Each of the planets has a different orbital path which means that they never bump into each other and they are each a different distance from the Sun.

MERCURY

Mercury is the closest planet to the Sun. Mercury has little air to protect it from the Sun's heat, so the side facing the Sun is **scorched**. Mercury is a small planet, about a third of the width of Earth. The surface of Mercury has even more craters than the Moon.

VENUS

Venus is almost the same size as Earth. Venus is covered in swirls of pink and white cloud. Venus is the hottest planet in our Solar System. It is even hotter than Mercury because its clouds keep the Sun's heat in.

PLANET EARTH

Earth is about 150 million km away from the Sun. It has water on its surface and is the only planet known to have life on it. The Earth is made mostly of rock and is the **densest** planet in the Solar System.

17

MARS

Mars is made from rock and is covered in red dust. For this reason, it is sometimes called the 'Red Planet'. Mars is the only planet to have an atmosphere anything like Earth's. But Mars is a desert planet, it has no water. Valleys on Mars, however, show that water was once there in **abundance**.

JUPITER

Jupiter is by far the largest planet in the Solar System. It is a gigantic ball of gas, so is more similar to the Sun than to the Earth. Jupiter has more than 50 moons orbiting around it. The largest is named Ganymede and is larger than Mercury.

SATURN

Saturn is the second largest planet in the Solar System. It is another gas planet. Saturn has millions of pieces of rock and ice orbiting it, which makes it look as though it has rings around it.

URANUS

Uranus is so far from the Sun that it is a cold gas planet. It is made up of icy water, but mostly different types of gas, which gives the planet its blue colour. Uranus spins in a different direction to the other planets, which makes it seem as though it is spinning on its side. It is so far away from the Sun, that it takes Uranus 84 years to orbit it.

NEPTUNE

Neptune is the planet furthest away from the Sun. Like Uranus, it is a planet made mostly of gases and appears blue in colour. Neptune's moon, Triton, is even colder than the planet itself. It has volcanoes on its surface which erupt ice!

PLUTO

Pluto used to be known as the ninth planet, but in 2006, scientists reclassified it as a dwarf planet. Dwarf planets are like planets but much smaller. Pluto is even smaller than our moon. It has its own moon called Charon.

PERFECT PLANETS!

Venus is the brightest planet in our sky and can sometimes be seen without even using a telescope.

JUPITER

Jupiter is so big that you could fit all of the other planets inside it.

Neptune has the most stormy weather of all of the planets.

For a year or two every three **centuries**, Pluto's orbit means that it is actually closer to the Sun than Neptune.

THE STARS

The only star in our Solar System is the Sun, but we are able to see many more from where we are on Earth. Our Solar System is inside the Universe and there are millions of stars in the Universe.

OTHER SOLAR SYSTEMS

Like our sun, some other stars have solar systems of their own, meaning planets and other objects orbit around them. The further objects are away from our own planet, the less that scientists know about them.

GALAXIES

A group of stars is called a galaxy. The Sun is part of a galaxy called The Milky Way. The Milky Way is only one galaxy, but there are lots of galaxies in space. Galaxies are usually incredibly large and contain thousands of billions of stars.

THE MILKY WAY

SHAPING UP

Most galaxies are spiral in shape. The largest galaxies are called elliptical galaxies and are round in shape. Around one quarter of galaxies have no defined shape at all. These galaxies are called irregular galaxies.

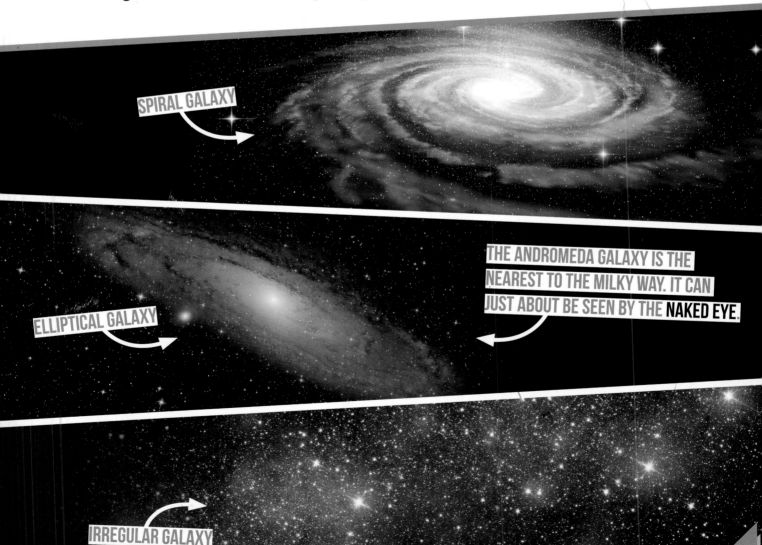

SPIRAL GALAXY

ELLIPTICAL GALAXY

THE ANDROMEDA GALAXY IS THE NEAREST TO THE MILKY WAY. IT CAN JUST ABOUT BE SEEN BY THE **NAKED EYE**.

IRREGULAR GALAXY

THE LIFE OF A STAR

All stars are formed in clouds of dust and gas called nebulae. Stars do not last forever, they burn until their fuel is used up. Depending on the size of the star, different things will happen when a star dies.

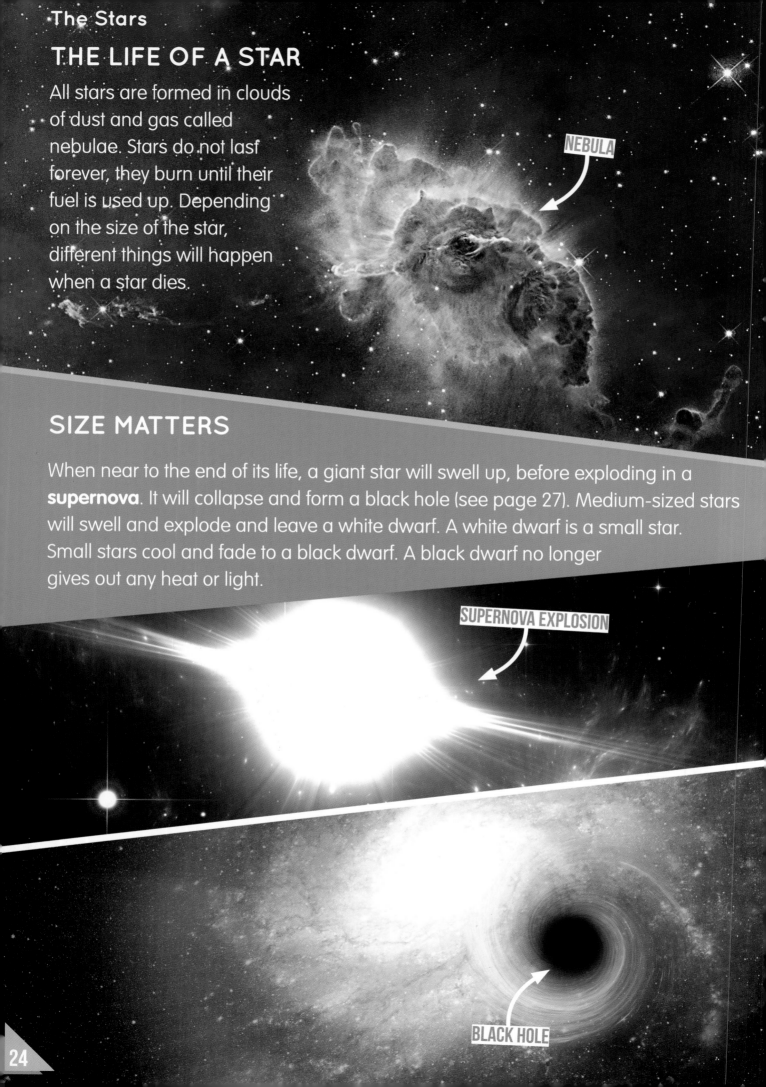

NEBULA

SIZE MATTERS

When near to the end of its life, a giant star will swell up, before exploding in a **supernova**. It will collapse and form a black hole (see page 27). Medium-sized stars will swell and explode and leave a white dwarf. A white dwarf is a small star. Small stars cool and fade to a black dwarf. A black dwarf no longer gives out any heat or light.

SUPERNOVA EXPLOSION

BLACK HOLE

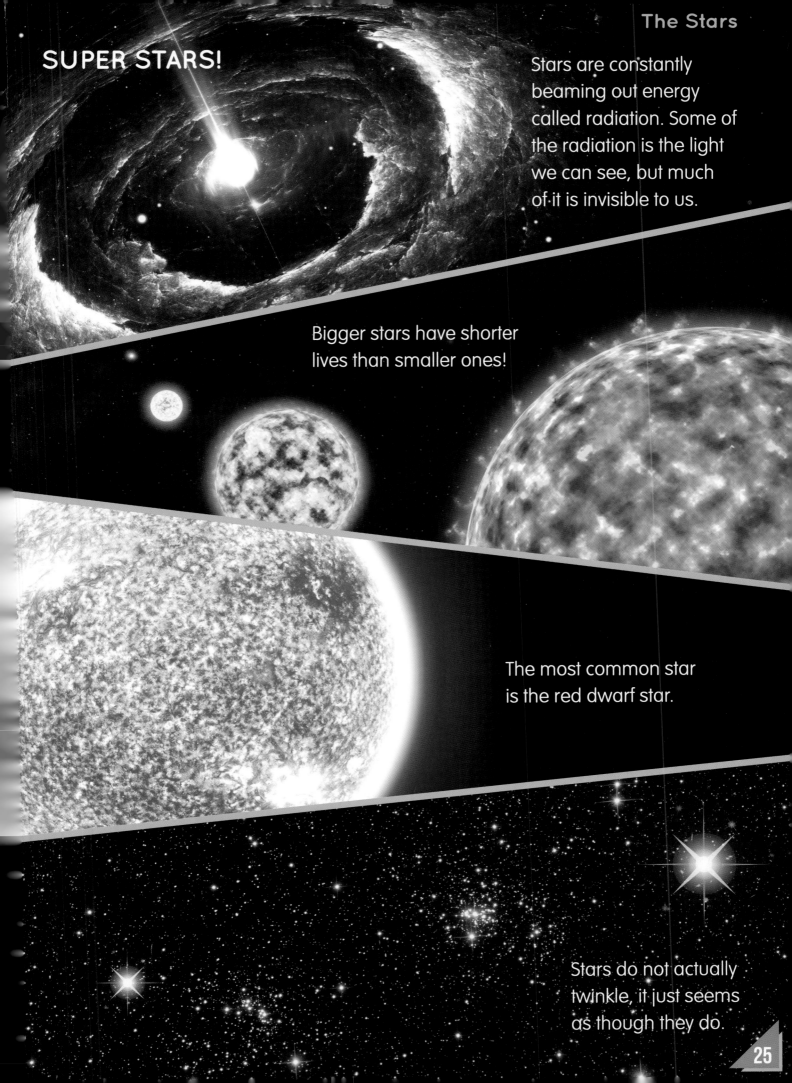

SUPER STARS!

Stars are constantly beaming out energy called radiation. Some of the radiation is the light we can see, but much of it is invisible to us.

Bigger stars have shorter lives than smaller ones!

The most common star is the red dwarf star.

Stars do not actually twinkle, it just seems as though they do.

WHAT ELSE IS OUT THERE?

The size of outer space is large and much of it is yet to be explored by Earth's scientists. Astronauts and astronomers are learning more and more all of the time and, as technology advances, they will continue to do so. So what else is out there that we do know about?

ASTEROIDS

Asteroids orbit the Sun like miniature planets. They are basically small pieces of rock that have broken off larger objects that have **collided**. Asteroids come in a variety of shapes and sizes. In order to learn more about them, space probes were sent to asteroids to send information back to Earth.

AN ASTEROID BELT IS A LARGE COLLECTION OF ASTEROIDS IN ORBIT TOGETHER.

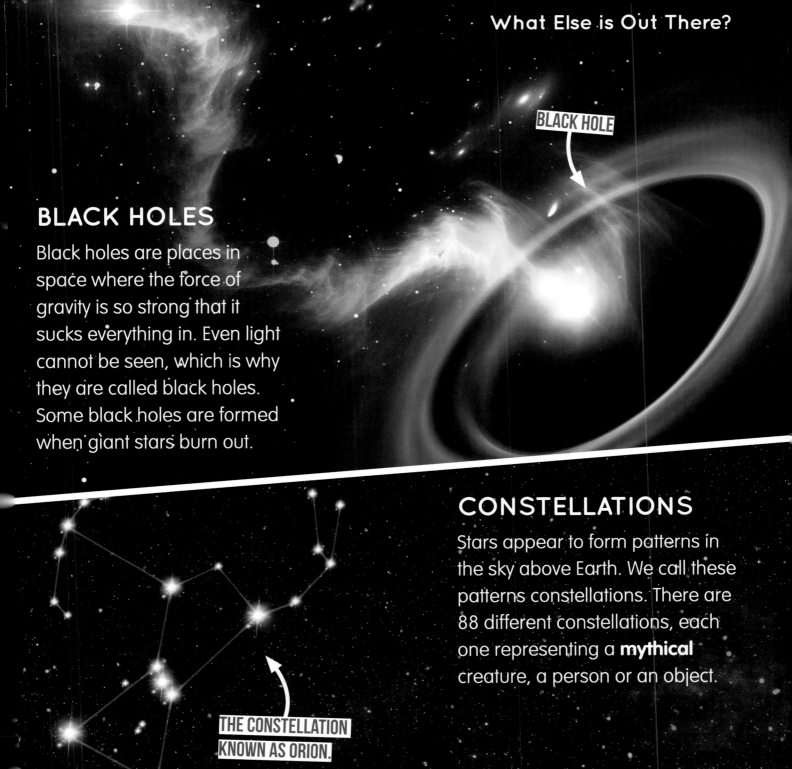

BLACK HOLE

BLACK HOLES

Black holes are places in space where the force of gravity is so strong that it sucks everything in. Even light cannot be seen, which is why they are called black holes. Some black holes are formed when giant stars burn out.

CONSTELLATIONS

Stars appear to form patterns in the sky above Earth. We call these patterns constellations. There are 88 different constellations, each one representing a **mythical** creature, a person or an object.

THE CONSTELLATION KNOWN AS ORION.

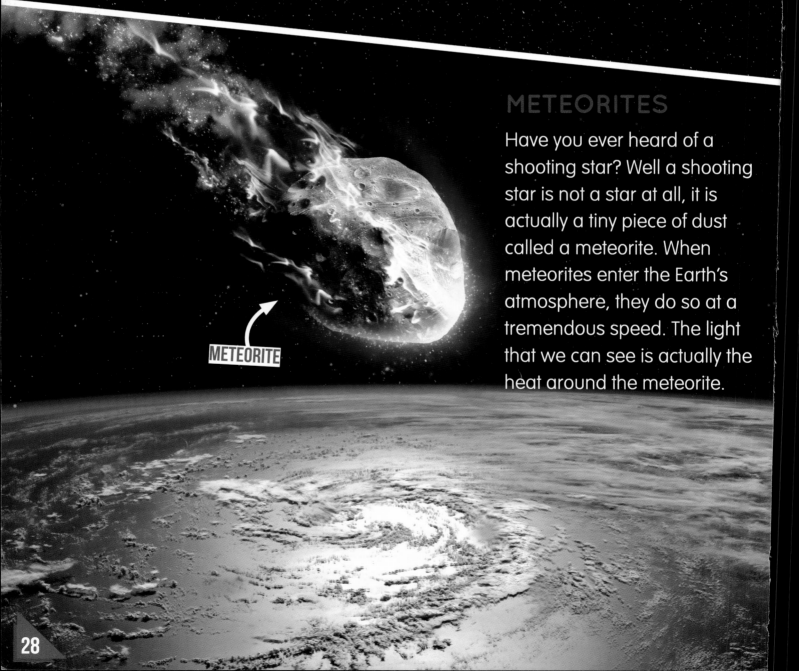

COMETS

COMET

Comets are one of the rarer sights in outer space. They are made up of dust and ice and come from the outskirts of the Solar System. Sometimes, a comet will travel inside the Solar System. When they do so, they begin to melt and leave tails trailing behind them.

METEORITES

Have you ever heard of a shooting star? Well a shooting star is not a star at all, it is actually a tiny piece of dust called a meteorite. When meteorites enter the Earth's atmosphere, they do so at a tremendous speed. The light that we can see is actually the heat around the meteorite.

METEORITE

SATELLITES

An artificial satellite is one sent into space by humans to orbit a planet. Satellites are held in place by gravity. They can be used to give humans useful information. Satellites can be used to watch the weather so that **meteorologists** can predict hurricanes and other types of weather. They can also be used to navigate cars, ships and aircrafts. Satellites are useful tools for teaching us more about space in general.

ARTIFICIAL SATELLITE

CAR SATELLITE NAVIGATION (CAR SAT NAV)

ALIEN LIFE?

Man has long since wondered whether our world is the only planet where life exists. Thus far, scientists are yet to find another planet remotely like ours. Life, as we know it, needs water and the right amount of heat. Scientists are always looking for water on other planets and moons.

IMAGINARY ALIENS

So fascinating has the thought of alien life always been, that many films and books include the existence of aliens. Sometimes they are evil characters who want to destroy Earth, on other occasions they come in peace. What do you think?

GLOSSARY

abundance	a very large quantity of something
axis	an imaginary line about which a body rotates
centuries	hundreds of years
collided	crashed into each other whilst moving
densest	heaviest
magnetic field	a layer which protects the Earth
mass	large matter with no definite shape
meteorologists	scientists who study weather
mythical	occurring in myths or folk tales
naked eye	without the use of enhancers such as telescopes
oxygen	part of the air which humans need to breathe
scorched	burnt
spherical	a 3D shape like a ball
supernova	a star that suddenly increases in brightness

INDEX